W9-BSX-382

GREAT AMERICAN MEMORIALS

THE Washington Monument

A BEACON FOR AMERICA

BRENT ASHABRANNER

*Photographs by Jennifer Ashabranner
and Historical Prints and Photographs*

Twenty-First Century Books　Brookfield, Connecticut

To the memory of
THOMAS LINCOLN CASEY
the man who built the Washington Monument

Published by Twenty-First Century Books
A Division of the Millbrook Press, Inc.
2 Old New Milford Road
Brookfield, Connecticut 06804
www.millbrookpress.com

Other photographs courtesy of: White House Collection: p. 4; Terry J. Adams/
National Park Service: p. 12; Library of Congress: pp. 17, 21, 23, 25, 28, 32, 34, 39, 43,
46, 49; © Corbis: p. 18; National Archives: pp. 42, 59; Smithsonian Institution: p. 51

Library of Congress Cataloging-in-Publication Data
Ashabranner, Brent K., 1921-
The Washington Monument : a beacon for America / Brent Ashabranner ;
photographs by Jennifer Ashabranner and historical photographs.
p. cm.— (Great American memorials)
Includes bibliographical references and index.
Summary: Chronicles the history of the monument that honors our first president,
discussing its design, financing, long period of construction, controversies, completion,
dedication, and symbolism.
ISBN 0-7613-1524-1 (lib. bdg.)
1. Washington Monument (Washington, D.C.)—History—Juvenile literature. 2. Wash-
ington Monument (Washington, D.C.)—Pictorial works—Juvenile literature. 3. Wash-
ington (D.C.)—Buildings, structures, etc.—Juvenile literature. [1. Washington Monument (Washington, D.C.) 2. National monuments.] I. Ashabranner, Jennifer, ill. II. Title.
F203.4.W3 A84 2002
975.3—dc21   2001052754

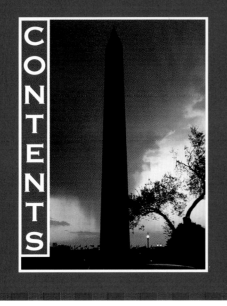

C
O
N
T
E
N
T
S

The name of

Washington

*will spread with liberty
from age to age.*

—François René Chateaubriand,
Nineteenth-Century
French Commentator on America

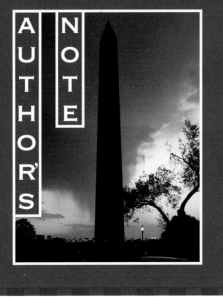

America's Birthday

T he Fourth of July is America's oldest national holiday. Every year Americans in cities, towns, and villages across the country celebrate the signing of the Declaration of Independence, which took place in Philadelphia on July 4, 1776. They celebrate with parades, picnics, patriotic speeches, and fireworks. This is Independence Day. This is America's birthday.

Washington, D.C., did not exist when the Declaration of Independence was signed. But in the more than two centuries since it became the capital of the United States, this city on the banks of the Potomac River has become the place to be on America's birthday. The celebration begins with a grand parade and ends with a spectacular fireworks display in the evening. In between, visitors picnic and play as they do all across the United States.

Jennifer and I were in Washington on July 4, 2001, the 225th anniversary of the signing of the Declaration of Independence. We were there with tens of thousands of other visitors, many of whom had traveled a long distance to take part in the celebration. Some dark clouds on the horizon did not dampen people's spirits as they crowded along Constitution Avenue to get a good spot for the parade.

Marching bands from many parts of the country participated in the 2001 Independence Day parade in Washington, D.C.

A GRAND PARADE

The parade begins at Seventh Street near the National Gallery of Art, goes down Constitution Avenue, which flanks the Mall on its north side, passes the Washington Monument, and ends near the Vietnam Veterans Memorial at Seventeenth Street.

As Jennifer and I walked down Constitution Avenue toward the Washington Monument, I looked at the people lining the curbs in anticipation of the parade. What I saw reminded me that the Fourth of July is not only our oldest national holiday; it has always also been a day of national unification—a time when political, religious, and ethnic dif-

Washington visitors wait patiently for the Fourth of July parade.

ferences are put aside and citizens unite as Americans. In the space of two blocks, I saw a wonderful cross-section of America: Hispanics, African Americans, whites, Native Americans, Arab Americans, women in Indian saris, others in the colorful dress of their former Asian homelands. Everyone was shouting, laughing, having a good time.

We found a good spot on Constitution Avenue, almost directly across from the Washington Monument. I have seen the Independence Day parade in our nation's capital several times, and I most enjoy seeing it against the backdrop of this sky-piercing white marble obelisk. Standing atop a gentle hill, surrounded by American flags, the simple but magnificent monument honors George Washington, commander of the Continental Army and first president of the United States. It has become our most visible reminder of the historic moment of our nation's founding. It is the symbolic heart of our democracy.

Red, white, and blue star balloons dress up the 2001 Fourth of July parade.

The crowd cheers as a father and son stilt team parades as Uncle Sam and Little Sam.

The rain clouds were still in the background, but the crowd waited patiently in the hot sun. We could hear the parade before we could see it. Then suddenly there it was, a river of music and color flowing past us: the Metropolitan D.C. Police Motorcycle Team and Honor Guard, a marching unit from the U.S. Army Military District of Washington, D.C., U.S. Navy marchers in their dazzling white uniforms. A

This 30-foot American bald eagle balloon makes a breathtaking swoop down the Constitution Avenue parade route.

great crowd favorite was Uncle Sam on stilts—at least 20 feet (6 meters) high—followed by Little Sam, a real father and son team. The Grand Marshall of the parade—Miss America 2001, Angela Perez Baraquio—rode in a huge convertible, waving to everyone.

I lost count of the number of high school bands marching proudly down Constitution Avenue playing "The Battle Hymn of the Republic" and marches like "Stars and Stripes Forever." They were there from cities and towns across America. The Military Order of the Purple Heart passed by, commemorating the sixtieth anniversary of Pearl Harbor. Vietnam War pilots stood at attention beside a helicopter pulled by a truck.

And there was fun, lots of it. The Texas Lone Star Cloggers from Dallas danced and twirled down the avenue, as did the Casco Bay Cloggers from South Portland Bay, Maine. Shriners dressed as clowns chased one another in tiny go-carts.

A circus calliope from Meigs County, Ohio, provided music. And so did the Boulder City Hometown Fiddlers from Henderson, Nevada.

The highlight of the parade for me was a 30-foot (9-meter) American bald eagle floating down Constitution Avenue. The giant helium balloon-bird was astonishingly lifelike, and I hardly noticed the ropes and the half dozen handlers hanging onto them.

SPECTACULAR FIREWORKS

When the last of the parade had passed, Jennifer and I crossed Constitution Avenue and walked up one of the paths to the Washington Monument. Many families had already made themselves comfortable on the monument grounds, settled for a day of fun and picnicking. Blankets were spread on the grass, beach umbrellas set up, even a few tents pitched. And some food baskets were already being unloaded.

Visitors settle on the Washington Monument grounds for a day of picnics and games as they wait for the evening fireworks display.

There are a number of good places on the Mall for a relaxed Fourth of July outing, but few can match the Washington Monument grounds for a view of the fireworks spectacular that the night will bring. The fireworks staging area is at the east end of the Reflecting Pool, very near the monument.

The monument grounds are expansive, especially the sweep of green that stretches toward the Lincoln Memorial, and provide plenty of room for people to play ball or toss Frisbees for their dogs to catch.

Holding Fourth of July celebrations in this area became a tradition during Thomas Jefferson's two terms as president, but the activities were a little different then. At the beginning of the nineteenth century, people came in swarms to watch horse races and contests of manly strength such as wrestling and log lifting. Public officials delivered long speeches, reminding their audience that freedom was worth fighting for. Businesses closed for the day, except for merchants who sold ice cream and fireworks.

The activities have changed in two hundred years, I thought as a blue Frisbee sailed over my head, but not much else.

About five o'clock the clouds moved in, and the rain fell intermittently throughout the evening. Many people who had come to watch the fireworks sought shelter between the columns of the Lincoln Memorial. Several hundred stood in the Jefferson Memorial where they could still get a good view of the aerial show that soon would burst over the Washington Monument. But most people who had staked out places on the grounds of the Washington Monument during the day stayed there, using beach umbrellas, tarps, or blankets as makeshift rain shelters. The few with tents generously shared their dry space.

Jennifer and I, relatively dry in rain gear, pushed our way into the expectant crowd around the Washington Monument. Everyone waited, hoping the fireworks display would not be postponed.

Fourth of July fireworks bursting over the Washington Monument

"Maybe we'll be lucky," a Hispanic man beside me said. We started talking, and I learned that the man and his wife, standing beside him, had become U.S. citizens that day, taking part in the traditional Fourth of July naturalization ceremony held in the District each year.

Shortly before nine o'clock the rain stopped, and the crowd got its wish—in just a few minutes the fireworks began. Instantly "shooting stars" filled the sky above the Washington Monument, and the crowd cheered. Some of the stars exploded in great balls of fire. The whole time a noise like a machine gun filled the night as countless shells shattered in the air. A light rain started again during the main part of the show, but it only seemed to increase the beauty of the dazzling patterns of fire in the sky. When the show ended, about twenty minutes after it began, the crowd was still shouting and applauding.

Before we left, I again congratulated the man beside me on becoming a United States citizen.

"Yes," he said, "it is good to be an American." He looked up at the Washington Monument and smiled as he added, "even a very wet American."

And, I thought, what more special place for a new American to be on Independence Day than standing beside the most revered symbol of his new homeland's freedom.

CHAPTER ONE

A Nation Is Born

The story of George Washington's role in America's fight for independence is familiar to all Americans.

For years the American colonists had been struggling to extricate themselves from tight British control. The colonists' grievances with Britain were many: laws that forced them to use only English ships and to sell their products only to English merchants; burdensome taxes that even the poorest had to pay; restrictions on the colonists' freedoms. Most serious, the English Parliament continued to ignore the lawmaking assemblies of the colonies. As tensions between the colonists and British grew, Britain sent troops into Boston and New York City. This angered the colonists.

In September 1774 the colonists formed a Continental Congress, which met in Philadelphia to consider action against the British. The delegates called for a boycott of British products until Britain repealed some of its restrictions on the colonists. King George refused, and in April British troops tried to seize the military supplies of the Massachusetts militia. The dark clouds of war were gathering. Colonial "Minutemen"—volunteers ready to fight at a minute's notice—skirmished with British troops at Lexington and Concord near Boston.

In May 1775 the Continental Congress, with delegates from each of the thirteen American colonies of Great Britain, met for a second time in Philadelphia. Among the members were John Hancock and John Adams of Massachusetts, Benjamin Franklin of Pennsylvania, and Thomas Jefferson and George Washington of Virginia. Their mission: to solve the colonies' problems with the King of England or, if they could not, to declare independence from the mother country.

One of the first actions of the Congress was the creation of a Continental Army, beginning with the approximately fifteen thousand ragtag volunteers who had poured into the Boston area. George Washington was unanimously chosen to command the new army, and he left immediately for Boston.

Many members of the Congress still hoped for peace with Great Britain, and over the next year they heatedly discussed the issues. During that time, in March 1776, the new Continental Army drove the British out of Boston. George Washington then moved his troops to New York, where the British were increasing their forces.

At last the moment of decision came. On July 1, 1776, the Continental Congress debated whether or not to declare independence from Britain. "The morning is assigned the greatest debate of all," John Adams wrote. "A declaration that these colonies are free and independent. . . . This day or tomorrow is to determine its fate." Adams delivered a powerful speech in favor of independence.

On July 2 the debate ended, and a vote was taken. The colonies voted for independence, 12–0, with New York abstaining. Congress discussed whether to sign a Declaration of Independence that had been drafted by Thomas Jefferson. Discussion continued on July 3 as delegates made changes in Jefferson's original wording.

On July 4 discussion ended and another vote was taken. By a vote of 12–0, with New York again abstaining, the delegates approved the Declaration of Independence. The Declaration was printed, and on July 8 it was read to a great cheering crowd in the Philadelphia State House yard. Bells rang all day; troops paraded in the streets; thirteen cannon blasts were fired, one for each colony that would now fight for independence.

Messengers on horseback carried copies of the Declaration throughout the colonies. In New York, General Washington assembled his troops, and the Declaration of Independence was read to each brigade. A celebrating New York crowd tore down a large equestrian statue of English King George III that stood in lower Manhattan. The Declaration was officially approved by New York.

A new nation, the United States of America, had been born. But it would take a long war to secure the new nation's future.

GEORGE WASHINGTON'S WAR

George Washington, as commander of the Continental Army, was charged with driving the British out of the country and securing the nation's independence.

Born and raised in the colony of Virginia, Washington had been an officer in the Virginia militia and had fought for the British in the French and Indian Wars. That military experience, however, was small preparation for the overwhelming task he undertook in 1775 as commander of the Continental Army. His small, untrained, poorly equipped, largely volunteer army would face the Royal Army of Great Britain, then the most powerful army on Earth.

Washington proved to be an inspired and inspiring military leader. In the long and bitter, often merciless War of Independence that followed, he organized and brought discipline to the colonial forces. He brought pressure on colonial governors to provide reinforcements, food, and clothes for his cold and hungry troops. He moved his small army around the country, surviving the worst blows of the British, learning from his mistakes, winning the battles that had to be won.

Always in the thick of battle, General George Washington leads his troops in the fight against the Hessians at Trenton, New Jersey.

Even as it raged, colonists called the struggle "George Washington's War." At last, after eight and a half long years, his unwavering leadership and his army's bravery brought victory and independence to the American colonies.

THE FIRST PRESIDENT

After the war Washington returned to his home state of Virginia, hoping to live a quiet life on his plantation, Mount Vernon. But it soon became apparent that the young republic, held together only by the weak Articles of Confederation that gave almost no power to the central government, was still in danger of breaking apart. In 1787 a Constitutional Convention was held in Philadelphia to try to establish a stronger federal government. Washington was reluctant to leave Mount Vernon, but he agreed to attend, saying, ". . . to see this nation happy . . . is so much the wish of my soul."

George Washington waves to the crowd celebrating his inauguration as the first president of the Unied States on April 30, 1789, in New York City.

Washington was elected president of the Constitutional Convention. After the Constitution was developed and ratified by the states, Washington was unanimously elected first president of the United States, taking office in 1789. With the same devotion to duty that he had shown throughout the long war, he worked to create an effective central government, supporting a national bank, taxation to pay federal expenses, and the strengthening of the army and navy. He gave much effort to developing foreign policy for the young nation, to solving the problems of westward expansion, and to adding new states to the Union.

At the end of his first term as president, Washington made known his wish to retire. Leaders of both political parties pleaded with him to reconsider. Without his leadership, they told him, the fragile nation might still break up. Thomas Jefferson was clearly frightened by the thought of Washington's retirement. "This is the event at which I tremble," he wrote Washington. "The confidence of the whole country is centered in you." Washington finally agreed to serve a second term and was reelected, again unanimously. But he firmly turned aside all pleas that he serve a third term. Now a living American legend, in 1797 he once more retired to Mount Vernon.

When George Washington died on December 14, 1799, the entire country went into mourning. A day after his funeral, the U.S. House of Representatives passed a resolution offered by Light-Horse Harry Lee, one of the gallant cavalry officers who had served with Washington during the Revolutionary War. The resolution praised the great leader and contained the words that we know so well today: "First in war, first in peace, and first in the hearts of his countrymen."

CHAPTER TWO

A Memorial for the Nation's Father

T he first resolution to create a memorial to honor George Washington was passed in 1783 by the Continental Congress in Philadelphia. Washington was still commander of the Continental Army, but the War of Independence had ended with the surrender of the British at Yorktown in 1781. Although the Congress was burdened with problems of an empty treasury, shaky foreign affairs, and rivalries between the states, the delegates knew that the American people were grateful for their freedom and firmly believed that they owed it to one man: George Washington.

The Continental Congress resolution called for erecting an equestrian statue of Washington. Washington would be clothed in Roman dress and holding a staff of victory in his right hand. The statue would be made of bronze and placed atop a marble pedestal. Despite its good intentions, however, the Continental Congress took no action to have the statue made.

By 1790 the new Congress of the United States, now meeting in New York, had selected a site for the country's capital city, to be called Washington. It would be built in a 10-mile-square area (100 square miles, 259 square kilometers) split by the Potomac River. The land would be ceded to the federal government by the states of Maryland and Virginia. (Eventually, only Maryland land was used.)

Pierre Charles L'Enfant, a talented French engineer who had fought for the colonies in the Revolutionary War and now lived in New York, was selected by George Washington to draw up a plan for the new capital. Working feverishly, L'Enfant submitted his design in 1791, so detailed that it even included the equestrian statue of Washington approved by the old Continental Congress. In his vision of the capital city, L'Enfant saw "a vast esplanade," a great grassy mall 400 feet (122 meters) wide that would run for about a mile directly from the yet-to-be-built Capitol and end at the statue of Washington. The statue would be located exactly where the

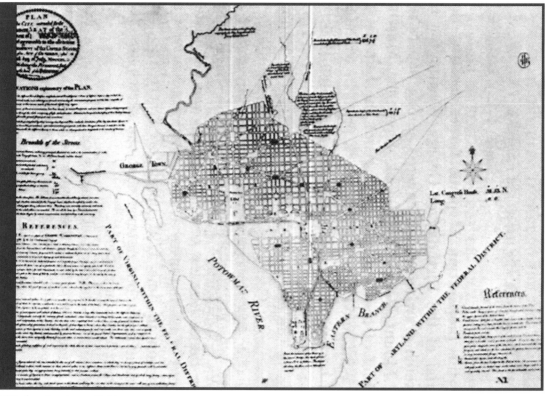

L'Enfant's plan, 1791

view from the Capitol intersected with the view southward from the yet-to-be-built president's mansion.

The city of Washington began to be laid out in the last decade of the century, work on the Capitol and the president's mansion (later to be called the White House) going forward. No action was taken to create the equestrian statue of George Washington, however. In fact, President Washington himself, in New York, let it be known that he wanted no time or money spent on a memorial to him while he was still alive.

But when Washington died in 1799, a saddened U.S. Congress met immediately to decide on a fitting memorial for the man who had led his country to freedom. Reaching a decision on what the memorial should be, however, proved to be bewilderingly difficult.

The government had now moved from New York to Washington, D.C. Some legislators wanted a marble statue of Washington placed in the Capitol and his body interred under it. Reluctantly, Martha Washington agreed that her husband's body could be moved from Mount Vernon. But others wanted an elaborate mausoleum to be built in the Capitol with a marble sarcophagus in the center to hold Washington's body. Still other legislators felt that the original idea of an equestrian statue was best.

The debates continued into the new century, and Congress passed no legislation for a Washington memorial. Soon the War of 1812, followed by years of national financial and political problems, prevented any serious consideration of a Washington memorial by Congress.

In 1832, however, legislators were again faced squarely with the question of a memorial. The hundredth anniversary of George Washington's birth was the perfect time to make a decision about a memorial. But once more Congress was unable to agree; no memorial legislation was passed.

It was now clear to the American public that, if left to Congress, a memorial honoring George Washington might never be built. Newspapers around the country criticized the lawmakers for their inability to act.

In that climate of unhappiness with Congress, a group of prominent citizens, led by Chief Justice of the Supreme Court John Marshall, formed the Washington National Monument Society in 1833 to devise a plan for getting a monument built. The Society began a nationwide campaign to raise money to build the monument. Collection agents were appointed in each state and territory of the United States.

Memory of Washington.

To the CITIZENS of the UNITED STATES.

WHEN your beloved WASHINGTON, THE FATHER OF HIS COUNTRY, died! You saw with increased sensibility the universe in tears! AMERICANS! How did your bosoms dilate and glow, when, at the first meeting of your political fathers, following the melancholly event, you saw the call for a MONUMENT worthy of the SUBLIME VIRTUES you hoped to perpetuate, universally applauded!

How then FELLOW COUNTRYMEN, have ye permitted two whole years to pass since the noble and natural resolution was every where individually formed; and the traveller still to ask in vain, *Where is* THE NATIONAL MONUMENT, *sacred to Public and Private Virtue; to the manes of the illustrious* WASHINGTON?

COLUMBIANS! You owe to the world, as well as to yourselves, an apology, or an explanation, for the mysterious delay of your acknowledged duty: Since nothing can be more true, than that a mere difference of opinion, respecting the form of the Monument, or the mode of its elevation, is the sole cause. To prove this, let us agree at once to obviate all difficulty, by uniting in a simple plan to accord with the annexed, *now in operation—*

Terms of Subscription,

To a MONUMENT *sacred to Public and Private Virtue, dedicated to GEORGE WASHINGTON, to be erected in the City bearing his name, by the voluntary contribution of citizens of the* United States only.—*The form, and inscriptions, to be under the intire direction of three Trustees.*

I. THESE articles of subscription for a Monument to WASHINGTON may be opened in any district or part of the United States, provided that none but citizens be allowed to subscribe, and that no individual be allowed to contribute in his own name more than one *Eagle,* (or *Ten Dollars)* to this subscription fund.

II. THE name of each subscriber shall be written in a book, and transmitted with the subscription monies to either Branch of the Bank of the United States.

III. To render the whole design as simple as may be, three trusty and well beloved friends, namely, BUSHROD WASHINGTON, and JOHN MARSHALL, Judges in the Supreme Court of the United States, and BENJAMIN STODDERT, late Secretary of the Navy of the United States, or any two of them, are hereby empowered and requested to carry the whole design into effect, in such manner as in their wisdom may be deemed most honorable to the memory of WASHINGTON.

IV. SHOULD the sum hereby collected be more than sufficient for a Monument or Mausoleum, *whatever the object of our respect may be called,* the Trustees are hereby requested to appropriate the surplus to increase the fund which WASHINGTON began when in his last will and testament he virtually laid the corner stone of a NATIONAL UNIVERSITY.

V. THE Trustees are hereby empowered and requested to draw the subscription monies from the Bank, in which they are deposited at discretion, and also to deposit the original subscription book, either with the remains of WASHINGTON, or in the Library of the *National University,* founded by WASHINGTON. They are also requested to publish whenever they may think fit, statements of their progress in the important work, hereby consigned to their care.

An early appeal for money to build a monument to George Washington

At first, contributions were limited to one dollar per person per year. The idea behind this limitation was to involve as many Americans as possible in the building of the Washington Monument. The Society soon discovered, however, that they could not raise enough money that way. The contribution limit was removed, and other fund-raising activities were started. These included making appeals to schoolchildren and women's organizations, placing contribution boxes in post offices, and circulating contribution forms. But the monument fund still grew too slowly.

To further spur public enthusiasm, the Society decided the time had come to select a design for the Washington Monument. In 1836 the Society published a notice inviting American architects and artists to submit designs for a monument that would cost at least $1 million. There was only one guideline: The plan should "harmoniously blend durability, simplicity, and grandeur."

ROBERT MILLS, ARCHITECT

The response was excellent. After reviewing a great number of submissions, the Society selected a design submitted by Robert Mills, an architect with an impressive background. He was a former student of Benjamin Henry Latrobe, considered to be the first professional architect in the United States. Mills had designed many federal buildings in Washington, D.C., and in 1836 became Architect of Public Buildings in Washington, a position he held for the next fifteen years. Most relevant, Mills had already, in 1814, designed a monument in honor of George Washington for the nearby city of Baltimore. For the Baltimore monument, Mills had designed a tall Greek column 160 feet (48.8 meters) high surmounted by a statue of Washington.

For the monument in the nation's capital, Mills's design blended Greek and Egyptian architecture, consistent with the classical tastes of the period. Monumental in scope, the

The Robert Mills design for the Washington Monument

design included a grand circular colonnaded building like a Greek temple (pantheon) 250 feet (76 meters) in diameter and 100 feet (30 meters) high. Above the roof of the pantheon, he proposed a towering obelisk of 500 feet (152 meters), making the entire structure 600 feet (182 meters) high. The obelisk would be 70 square feet (6.5 square meters) at the base, tapering to 40 square feet (3.7 square meters).

There would be a 20-square-foot (1.8-square-meter) lookout at the top, "which opens a prospect all around the horizon." Mills's design for the circular building at the base was awesome. It included a 30-foot (9-meter) statue of George Washington dressed in a Roman toga and riding in a chariot drawn by six horses and driven by a mythical Winged Victory. Mills estimated that the cost of the monument would be $1,222,000.

By the end of 1838 the Washington National Monument Society had raised a total of $31,000 in contributions, a paltry sum considering how much was needed.

CHAPTER THREE

Construction Starts, Then Stops

The Washington National Monument Society's problems were not limited to disappointing contributions. Some early critics began to question Mills's design, calling it an "ill-assorted blend of Greek, Babylonian, and Egyptian architecture." This criticism further eroded public support for the monument.

Despite these problems, the Society pressed on with the plan. By 1848 contributions had reached $87,000, enough to begin work. But before beginning, the Society decided that they would build only the obelisk, fixing its height at 500 feet (152 meters). This decision was made both to save money and as a response to criticisms of the Mills design. The Society did not abandon the idea of a pantheon or some similar structure at the base of the obelisk. It simply left the possibility open for a future decision.

SITE SELECTION

Now the moment to select a site for the Washington Monument had arrived. The Society had always envisioned that the monument should be erected on the National Mall in

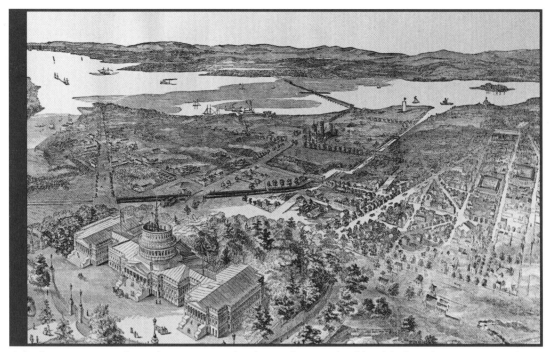

A balloonist's view of Washington in 1861 shows the stretch of land before the U.S. Capitol that would become the National Mall and the site of the Washington Monument.

Washington, D.C. But that required Congressional approval, and Congress was still debating the best kind of memorial to honor Washington. When the Society forced the issue by threatening to build the monument on private land, Congress finally agreed to a mall site.

The Society chose the location that L'Enfant had recommended more than half a century earlier—the point where the view westward from the Capitol intersected with the view southward from the White House. The final decision was to build the Washington Monument on higher grounds about 100 yards (91.4 meters) southeast of the exact intersection point.

The selection of this location was one of the Society's wisest and most important decisions. It placed the monument in what would become the symbolic center of the National Mall and on an elevation where the monument could be seen from all parts of Washington, D.C., and surrounding areas.

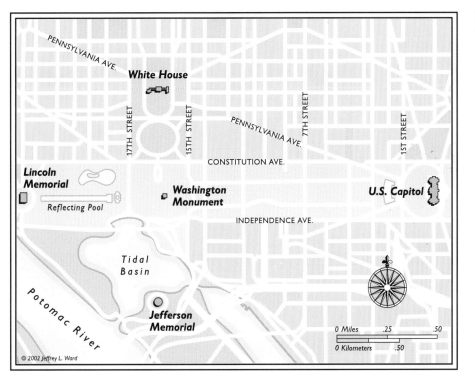

The National Mall today

CONSTRUCTION BEGINS

With the site of the monument now selected, the Society's building committee quickly put together a workforce: stonecutters to dress and polish the rough marble and other stone used, stonemasons to put it and other stone in place, carpenters, blacksmiths, ordinary laborers.

Stone was ordered, and wooden shelters were constructed to store it and to provide a place for the stonecutters to work. Rigs with ropes and pulleys for lifting blocks of stone were ordered. Later a steam engine was installed in a shed to provide power to stone-lifting cranes on top of the monument shaft.

Gneiss, a bluish granitelike stone, came from Potomac River quarries. The massive gneiss blocks, measuring 16 feet (4.9 meters) long, and 7 feet (2.1 meters) thick, were to be used for the foundation. The bluestone was delivered by scows to a Potomac River wharf. Rigs like the ones erected at the monument site hoisted the blocks onto wagons pulled by oxen. A road for hauling the stone had been built between the river wharf and the monument site.

From his quarry near Baltimore, Thomas Symington provided marble for the monument shaft. Before signing the contract, the building committee tested the marble and found that it could bear a pressure several times greater than it would sustain in any part of the finished monument.

Quarrying at the time was almost entirely a matter of manual strength against rock. (Pneumatic drills and hammers were not introduced until late in the nineteenth century, and mechanical diamond-tipped saws for cutting stone not until well into the twentieth century.) Explosives might sometimes be used to clear earth away from a seam or ledge of stone, but great care had to be taken not to cause cracks in the valuable stone.

At the Baltimore quarry, a line of workmen used long metal rods with chisel-like tips to separate a huge piece of marble from a seam. One workman would hold and rotate the rod while another struck it with a sledgehammer. When a crack appeared in the seam, wedges would be driven into the crack, and the great chunk of marble would fall free.

Quarriers called "breakers," using hammers and chisels, would then split the big piece of fallen marble into rough blocks approximately the size needed for the Washington Monument. The blocks were hauled on cars of the Susquehanna and Baltimore Railroad to an unloading dock near the monument. Later a railroad spur was built directly to the monument site.

Work on the foundation began in the spring of 1848. Explained Robert Mills:

> The foundation is built with massive stones of the firmest texture, the blue rock of the Potomac Valley, many of the blocks of which weigh from six to eight

tons. . . . The mortar used in bedding and binding the stones is composed of hydraulic cement and strong stone lime, with their proper proportion of coarse sand, which will become as hard as the stone it binds in a few weeks. . . . The square or footing of this foundation is eighty feet each way and rising by steps or offsets twenty-five feet high, the whole of solid masonry, upon which the obelisk shaft will be placed.

LAYING THE CORNERSTONE

The foundation was finished in a few months, and a ceremony to lay the cornerstone for the Washington Monument was held on July 4, 1848, to coincide with the celebration of the nation's seventy-second anniversary. The morning broke bright and clear, promising a perfect day to lay the cornerstone for the monument honoring the country's greatest hero and first president. The sound of church bells awakened the city. Guns fired salutes from the Washington Naval Yard. As the morning progressed, city residents filled the streets, and throngs of people from surrounding communities and rural areas poured into Washington. A reporter from the *Daily National Intelligencer,* Washington's leading newspaper, described the crowd in colorful language: "It were long to tell of the many bright-colored country bonnets which bustled and swayed about in the crowd, like poppy-heads shaken by the wind."

The greatest parade the city of Washington had yet seen made its way from the mustering grounds in front of the city hall toward the monument site: units from each branch of the military service in full dress, prancing cavalry horses, fire companies, carriages loaded with dignitaries, bands playing patriotic songs.

Festive decorations surrounded the monument site. Above an arch wrapped in colorful cotton, a tethered live bald eagle held the crowd in his piercing stare. It was not the first time this forty-year-old eagle had been part of a public

A sketch by artist J. J. Magee shows the grand procession for the laying of the Washington Monument cornerstone.

ceremony. He had greeted the French general Lafayette, who had fought for the colonies during the Revolutionary War, when he accepted a Congressional invitation to visit America in 1828.

Nearby, awning-covered seats had been placed for guests of honor. Besides President James K. Polk, guests included other government officials, military officers, representatives of foreign governments, officials from each state and territory, and a delegation of Cherokee, Chickasaw, Choctaw, and Creek Indians from the Indian Territory.

One guest was a little-known congressman from Illinois named Abraham Lincoln. The humble prairie lawyer who would become the sixteenth president of the United States had the utmost respect for the man who had founded the Union. In a speech in 1842, Lincoln said: "To add brightness to the sun, or glory to the name of Washington, is alike impossible."

Robert C. Winthrop, Speaker of the House of Representatives, gave the principal address at the ceremony. He spoke of the nation's debt to George Washington and said: "One tribute to his memory is left to be rendered . . . a national monument erected by the citizens of the United States of America. . . . Of such a monument we have come to lay the cornerstone. . . . The place is appropriate, here on the banks of his own beloved and beautiful Potomac."

Then came the laying of the cornerstone, a massive block of marble weighing 24,500 pounds (11,113 kilograms). Benjamin B. French, Grandmaster of the Masons in Washington, D.C., consecrated the cornerstone, using the same trowel that George Washington had used when the cornerstone of the U.S. Capitol was laid in 1793. After the consecration, workmen laid the cornerstone in the northeast corner of the foundation, the corner nearest both the U.S. Capitol and the White House.

The exciting day's events ended with a fireworks display at the Washington Naval Yard, the magnificence of which the capital's citizens had never before seen.

THE WORK CONTINUES

Construction of the shaft began in the fall of 1848. For the next six years the white marble obelisk rose slowly. When stone arrived at the monument, the rough blocks from the quarry had to be cut to specific size by the stonecutters. Gneiss used as interior backing for the marble had to be cut. Every block of marble had to be "dressed," a laborious process of smoothing and polishing the surfaces of the stones.

At that time, in some locations such as New York, steam-powered tools for dressing stones were beginning to replace the time-consuming manual process. The monument committee, however, rejected the use of mechanical tools and insisted that their stonecutters use the traditional manual methods. Reasons for this decision were never made clear but

This illustration from Gleason's Pictorial Drawing-Room Companion *shows artisans and stonecutters at work on the Washington Monument in 1853. Oxen were used to haul the heavy stone blocks to the site.*

probably stemmed from a belief that the old methods would result in a more beautiful tribute to George Washington.

Depending on their size and number, dressed stones were hauled from the stonecutters' sheds to the monument by oxen or by laborers pulling a "stone boat," a flat-bedded wooden sledlike carrier usually mounted on small wheels. Rigs and cranes hoisted the stones to the level where they were needed. Stonemasons called "layers" or "setters" placed the marble blocks in the monument shaft and set them in mortar. These specialists had laborers to assist them. A master mason directed the work and checked it for accuracy.

Although construction continued through this period, there were periodic slowdowns and worker layoffs when money was scarce. The problem of declining contributions continued to haunt the Washington National Monument Society.

In 1849 a group of Alabama citizens proposed to quarry and dress a block of marble from their state and present it to the Society as a gift for the interior wall of the monument. The Society accepted the stone and announced that it would accept a commemorative stone from each U.S. state and territory. All the stones would be fitted into the monument's interior wall. The Society believed the commemorative stones promoted patriotism and might encourage state contributions. While stones arrived from all of the states, they did not stimulate contributions.

Later, American Indian tribes, professional organizations, labor unions, businesses, individuals, and even foreign governments were permitted to donate memorial stones. One such stone—from the Vatican in Rome—caused a major problem.

In 1852 the Vatican informed the Society that Pope Pius IX, head of the Roman Catholic Church, would send a stone for the monument's interior wall. The stone was a block of marble originally from the Temple of Concord in Rome. Some anti-Catholic groups in America were outraged. They objected to the inclusion of a stone of religious significance in what was to be a secular monument. The strongest protests came from the Know-Nothing Party, a secretive, reactionary American political organization opposed to immigrants, particularly Roman Catholics, whom they blamed for many of the nation's economic woes. The Know-Nothings believed that only native-born Americans should be allowed to hold public office.

Despite the controversy, the Pope's stone arrived in Washington and was stored in one of the sheds on the mon-

THE STONECUTTERS

Artisans who cut and dress (smooth and polish) blocks of stone have been part of building history for thousands of years. Their skills have been essential to the construction of cathedrals, temples, palaces, and other great buildings in every part of the world. The stonecutters who worked on the Washington Monument from the 1840s to the 1880s used many techniques and tools that had been used for centuries. Cutting blocks of marble to the exact size needed was a laborious process. Frame saws were most often used for this work. The frame saw resembled the typical two-man wood-cutting saw except that its blade had no teeth. Its blade, made of smooth soft iron, was placed in a groove chiseled into the stone to be cut. An abrasive material, usually wet sand, was put in the groove, and the stone was cut by moving the iron blade back and forth over the sand, which little by little carved out the stone.

Once the marble block was cut to the proper size, it had to be dressed, work that required years of training and much skill. The rough surfaces of the block were leveled with a variety of chisels, picks, and hammers. Then the surfaces were brought to a smooth finish with an abrasive block of hard sandstone or some other kind of block and wet sand.

As the Washington Monument's marble walls rose, the number of stonecutters increased, outnumbering any other class of skilled workers. At one point almost one hundred stonecutters were at work on the monument.

Most stone cutting and dressing today is done by factory equipment; but the need for individual stonecutters still exists, especially in shaping stones for special purposes and artistic designs. The modern stonecutter is aided by diamond-tipped mechanical saws and pneumatic hammers, chisels, and polishers. But the work still requires a great deal of physical strength and as much skill as any stonecutter who ever worked on a twelfth-century cathedral.

ument grounds. In the early morning hours of March 6, 1854, intruders broke into the shed and stole the Pope's stone. It is believed that they threw it into the Potomac River, from which it was never recovered. No arrests were ever made, but the universal belief was that the thieves were members of the Know-Nothing Party.

This act of vandalism, carried out in the very shadow of what was to be a monument to George Washington, caused indignation across the nation. Catholics especially were out-raged, but millions of non-Catholics were also troubled by the political questions raised by the act. The Washington National Monument Society, caught in the middle of this anger and upset, suffered serious damage. As a result, contri-butions for building the monument decreased to a trickle.

CONSTRUCTION STOPS

By the end of 1854, the Society had again run out of money, and work on the Washington Monument came to a complete halt. At that time the shaft had risen to 152 feet (46.3 meters) and $230,000 had been spent on the monument. The theft of the Pope's stone had been a setback. Compounding the prob-lem, the nation seemed poised for a civil war. Few people were focused on a national monument.

The Washington National Monument Society now appealed to Congress for financial assistance. In February 1855, Henry May, chairman of the House committee consid-ering the request, made an impassioned plea to Congress for $200,000 to help the Society. For the first time Congress seemed ready to help.

Again it was the Know-Nothings who dealt the project a vicious blow. On the night of February 22, 1855, members of the Society who were also members of the Know-Noth-ing Party—or sympathetic to their views—called a surprise meeting of the Society. They elected new officers and a new board of managers and took all the Society records. The original officers and board protested bitterly, but for the next three years the two groups existed side by side. During those years, no contributions came in. Tools and machinery at the monument deteriorated. The group controlled by the Know-Nothings added 4 feet (1.2 meters) to the height of the Washington Monument during those years, but it used imperfect marble that had originally been rejected by the master mason.

Fortunately, the popularity of the Know-Nothings declined as fast as it had risen. By 1858 the old board regained control of the Washington National Monument Society. By this time, however, Congress was no longer considering giving money to help build the monument, and soon the nation was involved in the tragic Civil War. During the war years, the Society could only hope to preserve what had been completed and to keep the idea of a Washington Monument alive.

During the Civil War the city of Washington was in some ways like a huge Union Army camp. Within months after the First Battle of Bull Run, Washington had twenty-one hospitals scattered widely throughout the city to treat the wounded. Union soldiers drilled on the Washington Monument grounds. In 1861 the Union Army began to graze cattle on the grounds and built a slaughterhouse there to provide meat for the troops.

After the Civil War the Washington National Monument Society renewed its efforts to rally support for completing the monument, but failed dismally. One important newspaper, *The New York Herald*, called the unfinished monument a disgrace to the American people and urged its swift completion. In fact, many Americans, both Northerners and Southerners, wanted to see the monument completed. But in the stressful years following the war, putting broken lives and families back together took all of the nation's time and energy.

This cartoon titled the "Beef Depot Monument" satirizes the neglect that befell the Washington Monument during the Civil War as it stood unfinished. The grounds around the monument became a pasture for cattle and the site of a slaughterhouse.

The incomplete monument to George Washington stood for years, a neglected ugly stump on the landscape of the nation's capital. Far from being a proud tribute to America's greatest hero, the unfinished stack of marble blocks seemed a symbol of the bitterness and hatred that had divided the nation.

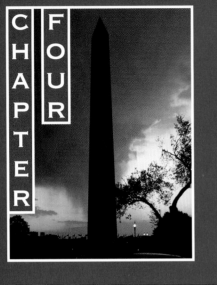

CHAPTER FOUR

The Slow Return to Construction

E arly in the 1870s the nation began to prepare for its centennial—the hundredth anniversary of American independence—which would be held on July 4, 1876. People throughout the country told their congressmen in Washington that the centennial would be a perfect time to dedicate a completed Washington Monument.

In January 1873 the U.S. House of Representatives appointed a committee to study the question of whether government money should be used to resume construction of the monument. Unfortunately, Congress did not act fast enough to make this happen, but in 1876 it did pass a $200,000 appropriation for the monument that would allow work to begin again. President Ulysses S. Grant approved the act on August 2, 1876.

Building the monument to George Washington was now the responsibility of the federal government, but the Society would serve in an advisory capacity.

For years, architects and engineers had raised questions about the soundness of the monument's design. Many believed the foundation would not support the weight of the gigantic marble obelisk. Before any newly appropriated money was spent on the monument, Congress appointed a Joint Commission on the Construction of the Washington Monument to look into the matter.

Working with a board of expert engineers, the Commission reached a disturbing conclusion: The stratum of sand and clay upon which the foundation rested was already loaded to the limit of safety. The Commission's report to Congress stated: ". . . it must be assumed that the foundation is insufficient to sustain the weight of the completed structure." Congress agreed and added $36,000 for strengthening the foundation to its original appropriation of $200,000.

A week later the Joint Commission, one of whose members was President Rutherford B. Hayes, made its most important decision. It appointed a career officer of the U.S. Army Corps of Engineers, Lieutenant Colonel Thomas Lincoln Casey, to take charge of building the Washington Monument.

A better choice for the daunting assignment is hard to imagine. Lieutenant Colonel Casey had graduated first in his class from West Point in 1852. He had rebuilt an important army fort on the East Coast. He had built roads and planned military reservations in Washington Territory. During the Civil War he had built coastal defenses in the state of Maine. He was a thoughtful planner, and he was a man of action.

Casey began his assignment by cleaning up the sadly neglected grounds around the monument stump. He repaired existing structures and built new carpenter, blacksmith, and stonecutter shops. He bought new tools and ordered machinery, particularly derricks for hoisting large stones. He built a

Lieutenant Colonel Thomas Lincoln Casey

road connecting the monument grounds to Fourteenth Street to help move supplies.

Now came the task of strengthening the monument's foundation. A number of architects and engineers in the past had given conflicting ideas on how to do this. Casey studied all these ideas and then developed his own plan.

Casey's plan called for two major steps. First, he would deepen the existing foundation and widen it so that the weight of the monument would be distributed over a larger area. Second, he would remove part of the old foundation from beneath the partially built shaft and then build concrete buttresses against all four sides of the monument to further support it.

Work on the monument's foundation progresses in August 1879.

The buttresses on the southeast side of the monument

The new foundation was completed in May 1880.

Despite bitter cold, work on strengthening the foundation began in February 1879. Deepening the foundation meant removing the earth from under the existing foundation and replacing it with a bed of concrete more than 13 feet (4 meters) thick. Lieutenant Colonel Casey was well aware of the skill and caution required for the task. To undermine a structure weighing 32,000 tons (29,030 metric tons), he said, was "a delicate operation."

His brilliant solution was to dig trenches 4 feet (1.2 meters) wide to the required depth under the existing foundation. The trenches would be dug in pairs, one on each side of the monument so that "unequal strain will not be brought on the structure." The trenches would then be filled with Portland cement. Additional pairs of trenches would be dug and filled until there was a solid slab of concrete as part of the monument foundation. The concrete slab would extend for 35 feet (10.7 meters) beyond the monument in each direction.

Casey needed workmen with experience in working underground to do the job, "men who do not mind the mud, darkness, and danger of such work," he said. He found some men with these qualifications in nearby Baltimore; they were tunnelers for a water supply system. The first phase of strengthening the monument foundation was completed by the end of October with no serious problems. The second phase had begun a month earlier. Workmen excavated 348 cubic yards (266 cubic meters) of earth from the old foundation and replaced it with cement for the buttresses that were built against the monument walls. Casey used a very strong concrete so that the buttresses would give maximum support and reinforcement.

The strengthened foundation was a piece of work that Lieutenant Colonel Casey could be proud of. It covered two and a half times as much area and extended 13.5 feet (4 meters) deeper than the old foundation. No damage had been done to the monument, not the slightest crack in any block of marble. And the job had been completed for less money than Congress had appropriated for the work.

CHAPTER FIVE

Completion and Dedication

The new foundation was finished, but Casey's task was just beginning. Work could now begin anew on the monument stump that had sat untouched for twenty-five years, but a crucial question remained unanswered. What should the Washington Monument look like?

The debate about its best design had never been resolved. And now architectural tastes had changed. People of the late nineteenth century (called the Victorian period for British Queen Victoria) preferred structural designs that were intricate, ornate, and complex over those that were simple.

Henry van Brunt, a prominent American architect of the time, said of the original design, "No person interested in our reputation as a civilized people can contemplate this completion without pain." A number of architects, artists, and influential public persons agreed with him and suggested that the unfinished monument should be demolished and that a new one designed in a more Victorian style should take its place.

An elaborate, almost cathedral-like design by William Wetmore Story, a well-known American sculptor, received special attention. Even the Washington National Monument

William Wetmore Story

John Froze

M. P. Hapwood

H. R. Searle

Paul Schulze

Some of the alternative designs for the monument suggested by Victorian architects

Society, which had always stood by the original design, began to support the Story design.

Nevertheless, the Mills design continued to have its admirers, not the least of which was the House of Representatives Washington Monument Committee, which said in 1873, "This rich and massive shaft, though simple and plain, would be a noble monument" to George Washington.

Thomas Lincoln Casey was an engineer, not an architect or art critic, and he did not let himself be drawn into the design controversy. He decided to stick with the original design until he was told otherwise. The only thing Casey excluded from his planning was a pantheon at the base of the obelisk, an idea that had been abandoned long before. But Casey did wonder about the design of the obelisk. Here he received important help from an unexpected source—George Perkins Marsh, the American ambassador to Italy at that time, and an authority on Egyptian obelisks.

Marsh's studies had shown that the height of an Egyptian obelisk was ten times the width of its base. Marsh's calculations also told him that the dimensions of the shaft should be reduced as it rose, the top of the obelisk varying from two thirds to three fourths of the length of the base. Casey absorbed all this information and much more as he worked on technical design problems with Ambassador Marsh.

Mills's original design had projected a relatively flat top for the shaft. Casey's plan was to make the monument a true obelisk, ending with a pyramidion, as the pyramid-shaped top of an Egyptian obelisk is called. Again, Marsh helped Casey figure the exact pyramidion dimensions for the Washington Monument.

When Casey finished his design, he presented it to the Joint Commission on the Construction of the Washington Monument and the Washington National Monument Society. Both organizations approved Casey's design and forwarded it to Congress with their strong recommendation. In a letter to Congress, Robert C. Winthrop, president of the Society, said:

. . . [the monument] was not undertaken to illustrate the fine arts of any period, but to commemorate the foremost man of all the ages . . . a simple, sublime shaft . . . rising nearer to the skies than any known on earth, will be no unworthy memorial, or inappropriate emblem, of his own exalted character and pre-eminent services.

Congress quickly approved the design.

CONSTRUCTING THE SHAFT

Meanwhile Casey had been busy ordering marble and making other construction decisions about the obelisk. He was most concerned about the quality of the marble that would be used. Here is part of his specifications to possible marble suppliers:

The marble must be white, strong, sound, and free from flint, shakes, powder cracks, or seams, and must in texture and color so conform to the marble now built in the monument as not to present any marked or striking contrast in color, luster, or shade, when set in the wall. . . .

Casey's goal of finding marble that perfectly matched the marble used earlier in the monument proved unachievable. The new marble, which came from a quarry near the Baltimore quarry that had supplied the original marble, was from a different stratum and was slightly different in color. The subtle color changes do not detract from the overall beauty of the monument, but they can be seen clearly beginning at the 150-foot (45.7-meter) mark, about where construction of the monument had stopped in 1854.

Casey decided to use granite for the backing of the monument's interior marble walls instead of the gneiss bluestone that had been used earlier. According to Casey's design, the granite backing would be reduced in thickness as the monument rose and would end at the 450-foot (137-meter) level.

From that point the obelisk would be entirely marble. Casey had no difficulty obtaining high-quality granite from several suppliers in Maine.

Before work on the shaft began, Casey had an iron framework built for the interior well of the monument. The framework, produced by the Phoenix Iron Company of Phoenixville, Pennsylvania, was to support an iron staircase and platforms that would reach to the top of the monument. I-beams and channel bars were strongly fastened into the columns of the framework, which rose in advance of the walls of the monument. In that way the framework could support the machinery needed for hoisting the marble and granite blocks.

Casey also installed a hoist with an engine powerful enough to lift a load of 10 tons (9 metric tons) at 50 feet (15 meters) per minute. The cables to pull the car were made of the best annealed steel wire. The winding drum held 500 feet (152 meters) of cable. It was Casey's idea that in the future the hoist would be converted to an elevator to carry passengers to the top of the monument.

Workmen hoist a piece of marble into place with the help of a stone-setting crane atop the monument.

In mid-July 1880, Casey began work on the obelisk. The first step was to remove the top 6 feet (1.8 meters) of the monument stump because Casey strongly felt that the 4 feet (1.2 meters) of inferior and damaged marble added by the Know-Nothings over twenty years earlier had to be taken out. He also believed that, for structural reasons in preparing the strongest base for the new marble, another 2 feet (.6 meters) of the old stone should be removed, reducing the monument shaft at that point to the 150-foot (45.7-meter) level.

The marble to be added from that point would be prepared according to the design Casey had worked out with Marsh. The shaft would taper ¼ inch to the foot (.64 centimeters to the meter) as it rose. The walls would attenuate (become thinner) from 15 feet (4.6 meters) at the base to 18 inches (45.7 centimeters) at the top of the shaft. The width at the base of the shaft was 55.5 feet (16.8 meters). The width at the top of the shaft would be 34.5 feet (10.5 meters).

On Saturday, August 7, 1880, another cornerstone-laying ceremony was held to mark resumption of work on the Washington Monument shaft. The hoist carried President and Mrs. Hayes and Lieutenant Colonel Casey to the 150-foot level. Before the new marble block was set, President Hayes placed in the cement a small coin with his initials and the date scratched on it.

By the end of the year Casey and his crew had raised the monument to 176 feet (53.6 meters). Another 74 feet (22.6 meters) were added in 1881, and by November of 1882 the obelisk had reached 340 feet (103.6 meters). The major part of the workforce now consisted of stonecutters. Their number grew from forty in July 1880 to more than one hundred when the work was in full swing.

The hard-driving Casey had a construction schedule that he was determined to keep, and he was sometimes frustrated by shipping delays. He had little tolerance for work stoppages, yet he showed understanding of worker demands

The monument shaft nears completion, but the crowning pyramidion is yet to be built.

and dealt successfully with several strikes by the strong stonecutters union.

Casey also showed a genuine concern for the welfare of his workers that was not common in supervisors in the nineteenth century. He had a safety net stretched around all sides of the monument, raising it as the work progressed. The net saved several lives during the course of the obelisk's construction. During Casey's years as supervisor, no crewmember died of an injury, either on the shaft or working underground on the foundation. Casey even provided hot coffee "in moderate amounts" for the men working at the top of the monument in cold weather.

Each November, Casey gave Congress a financial accounting of how he had spent the money appropriated for the Washington Monument and how much he needed to continue the work. Congress, with few exceptions, provided the money he asked for. The final cost of the monument was $1,187,710, a modest cost even in the nineteenth century. (Almost exactly a century later, the Vietnam Veterans Memorial cost more than $8 million.)

Construction proceeded on schedule throughout 1883 and the first half of 1884. On August 9 masons set the last piece of marble in place at the 500-foot level. The shaft was now finished, and only construction of the small pyramid-shaped obelisk roof, the pyramidion, remained to complete the Washington Monument.

According to Ambassador Marsh's calculations, the height of an Egyptian obelisk pyramidion should be the same as the width of the obelisk's base. Casey followed those guidelines and designed the Washington Monument's pyramidion to be 55 feet (16.8 meters) high. The pyramidion weighs 300 tons (272 metric tons) and is made up of 262 pieces of marble. To lighten the weight of the pyramidion, stonecutters pared the marble slabs to a thickness of 7 inches (17.8 centimeters). The slabs are supported by twelve marble ribs. The ribs, three on each side of the shaft, spring from the 470-foot (143-meter) level and converge at the top of the pyramidion.

The pyramidion has eight rectangular windows, two on each side. Ambassador Marsh was not happy with windows because a classical obelisk does not have them, but he understood that the Washington Monument would have visitors who would want to enjoy the view from that great height. Casey followed Marsh's advice to cover the windows with marble-slab shutters that pivoted on bronze hinges and could be opened and closed as needed. (In 1975 the windows were fitted with bulletproof glass).

As a final touch, stonecutters shaped a marble capstone for the pyramidion that weighed 3,300 pounds (1,497 kilograms). For the apex of the capstone Casey designed an aluminum cap 8.9 inches (22.6 centimeters) in length. The metal cap would serve as an integral part of a system of lightning rods for the monument. In the late nineteenth century, aluminum was a precious metal, and the little cap for the monument was the largest piece ever cast at that time. Casey was especially pleased because the aluminum would not tarnish when exposed to the weather, and thus would not stain the marble.

A cold rain fell in Washington, D.C., on the afternoon of December 6, 1884, but no rain could dampen the spirits of the small group of dignitaries on the platform at the top of the Washington Monument. As cannons roared a salute below and an American flag was unfurled atop the pyramidion, Lieutenant Colonel Casey had the honor, by means of ropes and pulley, of setting the capstone in place. Thirty-seven years after the first cornerstone had been laid, the monument honoring George Washington was complete.

The Washington Mounment today. Note the slight change in color at the 150-foot level.

The Washington Monument was dedicated on February 21, 1885, the day before George Washington's birthday. Snow covered the ground around the base of the monument and an icy wind swept off the Potomac River, but the day was clear. Many people braved the frigid weather, and the pavilion that had been set up for invited guests was full. The president of the United States, Chester A. Arthur, was in the place of honor.

Several dignitaries spoke, but the day truly belonged to Thomas Lincoln Casey, who did no more than describe the monument he had completed, talking with quiet pride about the strength of the foundation and the beauty of the monument itself. And then, turning to the president, Casey said, "For and in behalf of the Joint Commission for the Completion of the Washington Monument, I deliver to you this column."

President Arthur concluded the ceremony by declaring the monument dedicated "to the immortal name and memory of George Washington."

CHAPTER SIX

The Beacon in America's Front Yard

Today it is difficult for us to imagine that, even as it was being built, some architects called the Washington Monument "heathenish." Others wanted it replaced by a structure much more ornate, and one U.S. senator called it a "blot upon architecture." Now, after more than a century, most visitors see it for what it truly is: a shining symbol of America's independence.

From the moment of its completion and dedication in 1885, the sky-piercing monument quickly became one of the most visual symbols of the United States, not only for Americans but for people around the world. Americans throughout the country took pride in it and large numbers of visitors came to see it, many preferring to climb the 898 steps to the top even after the elevator began to carry visitors in 1887. By the end of the nineteenth century, 1,696,718 visitors had seen the breathtaking view from the 500-foot (152-meter) observation platform. In its pride, Congress mandated that the Washington Monument would always be the highest structure in Washington, D.C.

The view in every direction from the top of the monument offers an exciting look at our nation's capital, and each view has grown more beautiful and filled with history as the

View from Arlington National Cemetery　　　　*View from the Vietnam Veterans Memorial*

Views of the Washington Monument, which stands like a great beacon in the center of the National Mall in Washington, D.C.

View from the Lincoln Memorial

years have passed. Today, from the western windows, visitors can see the Lincoln Memorial, the Vietnam Veterans Memorial, the Korean War Veterans Memorial, and the Reflecting Pool together in their matchless unity. Beyond the Lincoln Memorial and the Potomac River, Arlington National Cemetery stands clearly against the Virginia skyline.

To the east, the view is filled with the green sweep of the National Mall, the Smithsonian Castle and the great museums, the Ulysses S. Grant Memorial, and—on the hill behind Grant's statue—the Capitol of the United States. To the north, the White House stands out with dramatic clarity. From the south windows, visitors see the Tidal Basin and the Jefferson Memorial with its wide ring of Japanese cherry trees. The trees, the water, the lovely white memorial standing apart form a serene picture, and on summer days people enjoying the Tidal Basin in paddleboats add to the charm.

Views from the Washington Monument

he Lincoln Memorial and the Reflecting Pool

The Jefferson Memorial

A MONUMENT FOR THE TWENTY-FIRST CENTURY

To be ready for the twenty-first century, the Washington Monument has undergone extensive rehabilitation both outside and inside. The work began in 1996 and required twenty stonemasons and other skilled workers. Their efforts included repairing 1,000 square feet (93 square meters) of chipped and patched stone, sealing 500 feet (152 meters) of exterior and interior stone cracks, pointing 64,000 linear feet (19,507 meters) of exterior joints (replacing crumbling mortar between marble blocks), cleaning 59,000 square feet (5,481 square meters) of interior wall surface, restoning 192 interior commemorative stones, sealing 8 observation windows, and installing 8 aircraft warning lights.

Other important inside work included upgrading the heating and air-conditioning systems as well as the elevator, and improving and enlarging the observation level. Newly installed floor-to-ceiling panels at the 490-foot (149-meter) exhibit level portray important events in George Washington's life and milestones in building the Washington Monument. Other exhibits include a replica of the aluminum apex of the monument's pyramidion and an original 1840s donation box for contributions to build the monument.

Famous American architect Michael Graves designed a decorative fabric sheathing—lit by interior lights—to disguise the scaffolding around the Washington Monument during its repair in the late 1990s.

A quarter of a million people gathered on the grounds between the Washington Monument and the Lincoln Memorial to hear Dr. Martin Luther King, Jr., deliver his famous "I Have a Dream" speech in 1963.

Now the Washington Monument stands as a beacon in America's Front Yard, as the Mall has become known. The spacious grounds around the monument provide the space every year for many cultural happenings: the African-American Family Reunion, jazz and military concerts, kite-flying contests, revival meetings. Sometimes the Washington Monument is a rallying point for the expression of American feelings: Martin Luther King's March on Washington for Jobs and Freedom, the anti–Vietnam War marches of the 1970s, the Million Mom March for gun control, and many more statements of the ideas and ideals of a free people. They are expressions of American life, and the Washington Monument looks over them all.

As the twenty-first century begins with a new kind of war—a war against terrorism—the Washington Monument will remind us that freedom must be fought for, and that, working together as a united people, Americans can defeat any enemy of freedom.

Information About the Washington Monument

- At a height of 555 feet 5⅛ inches (169.4 meters), the Washington Monument is the tallest freestanding all-masonry structure in the world.

- Total original cost of the building: $1,187,710

- Width at base of shaft: 55.5 feet (16.8 meters)

- Width at top of shaft: 34.5 feet (10.5 meters)

- Thickness of walls at base of shaft: 15 feet (4.6 meters)

- Thickness of walls at top of shaft: 18 inches (45.7 centimeters)

- Depth of foundation: 36 feet 10 inches (11 meters)

- Weight of monument: 81,120 tons (73,575 metric tons)

- Sway of monument in 30-mile-per-hour (48.3-kilometer-per-hour) wind: 0.125 of an inch (.32 centimeters)

- 897 steps in staircase to top (originally 898)

- Visibility from observation deck can reach more than 40 miles (64 kilometers) on a clear day.

Summer hours for going to the top of the Washington Monument begin the first Sunday in April, and the monument is open from 8:00 A.M. to 11:45 P.M. (Note: On the Fourth of July visiting hours are from 8:00 A.M. to noon.) Winter hours begin the day after Labor Day, and the monument is open 9:00 A.M. to 4:45 P.M.

Tickets are required to enter the monument. Free tickets can be obtained at the kiosk on the Fifteenth Street side of the monument. Advance tickets can be obtained through the National Parks Service at 1-800-967-2283 or at www.reservations.nps.gov. There is a $1.50 convenience charge per ticket and a $.50 handling fee per order.

Those interested in other information about the Washington Monument should contact the National Parks Service at:

National Capital Parks—Central
900 Ohio Drive, SW
Washington, D.C. 20024
Telephone: (202) 426-6841
Internet: www.nps.gov

Bibliography

Allen, Thomas B. *The Washington Monument: It Stands for All.* New York: Discovery Books, 2000.

Ancona, George. *Cutters, Carvers, and the Cathedral.* New York: Lothrop, Lee & Shepard Books, 1995.

Ashabranner, Brent. *On the Mall in Washington, D.C.: A Visit to America's Front Yard.* Brookfield, CT: Twenty-First Century Books, 2001.

Carroll, John Alexander. *George Washington.* New York: Charles Scribner's Sons, 1957.

Crane, Frank. "The Old-Time Fourth," *Outlook,* June 20, 1876.

Flexner, James Thomas. *Washington, the Indispensable Man.* Boston: Little, Brown & Company, 1969.

Gallagher, H. Pierce. "Robert Mills, 1781–1855: America's First Native Architect," *The Architectural Record,* May 1929.

Green, Constance McLaughlin. *Washington, Village and Capital, 1800–1878.* Princeton: Princeton University Press, 1962.

Harvey, Frederick L. *History of the Washington National Monument and the Washington National Monument Society.* 57th Congress, 2nd Session, Document No. 224, Washington, D.C.: GPO, 1903.

Hoig, Stan. *A Capital for the Nation*. New York: Cobblehill Books, 1990.

———. *It's the Fourth of July!* New York: Cobblehill Books, 1995.

Marrin, Albert. *George Washington and the Founding of a Nation*. New York: Dutton, 2001.

McCombs, Phil. "The Real Greatest Generation," *The Washington Post*, July 1, 2001.

McKee, Harley J. *Introduction to Early American Masonry*. Washington, D.C.: National Trust for Historic Preservation and Columbia University, 1977.

Torres, Louis. *"To the immortal name and memory of George Washington": The United States Army Corps of Engineers and the Construction of the Washington Monument*. Washington, D.C.: U.S. Army Corps of Engineers, 1984.

Vanhooser, Cassandra M. "A Capital Celebration," *Southern Living*, July 2001.

Index

Page numbers in *italics* refer to illustrations.